The Little
Miró

Catherine de Duve

A journey into the universe of the famou

KATE'ART
EDITIONS

Miró's

Joy

Strong colours, stars, crescent moons, constellations, comets, birds, fish, suns, Spanish dancers, magic… A ladder to escape to the sky. Miró's universe is full of surprises! And lots of joy!

Small Universe

War

In the 1930s, the rise of the *far-right* in Europe creates a climate of fear and insecurity. 1936 sees the start of a long and brutal civil war in Spain. Many artists have to leave the country. They must fight or flee the country! For both Miró and his friend Picasso, the exile is long and painful. At the end of the civil war in 1939, the winner, General Franco, establishes a powerful *dictatorship*.

Far-right: *far-right politics reject social equality and democratic principles and generally promote nationalistic and authoritarian regimes.*

Dictatorship: *Francisco Franco was a dictator. He remained in power until his death in 1975, when Juan Carlos was proclaimed King of Spain.*

Joan Miró

Joan Miró i Ferrà was born on April 20, 1893 in Barcelona, Spain. His father is a watchmaker and goldsmith and his mother, the daughter of a *cabinet-maker*. Joan has a younger sister, Dolorès. Joan spends his childhood in the heart of the *gothic* quarter of Barcelona, but he spends most of his holidays with his grandparents in the countryside in Catalonia and in Palma de Mallorca. There, little Joan can admire colourful landscapes and discovers nature and its wealth of insects and animals.

All his life he will keep vivid memories of his stays at the farm. Later, he will paint this fantastic farm in the moonlight. It is for him a "source of vital energy".

Can you spot the goat, the rooster and the rabbits in the barn? Where are the cart, the donkey and the dog?

As a child, his sketchbook and crayons are never far away. When he's only eight years old, he starts to draw snakes, peacocks, turtles, crickets…and just about everything else around him. He creates a *bestiary*.

Cabinet-maker: a craftsman specialising in making wooden furniture, chairs, etc.
Gothic: an architectural style typical of the Middle Ages (around the 12th century).
Bestiary: a book with writings or drawings of animals.

Create your own bestiary, just like Miro.
Draw your favourite farm animals!

Village

At 14, Joan enrols as a student at the School of Industrial and Fine Arts of Barcelona. One of his teachers, a friend of the famous French realist painter Gustave Courbet, tells him about Paris... But Joan's father wants him to study business. At 17, Joan has to work as an accounts clerk in a drugstore… This kind of job does not suit him at all! He falls ill as a result and must spend time recovering at his parents' farm in Mont-Roig.

Observe the Catalan landscape, the village and its surrounding fields. What do the abstract shapes represent?

Exhibition

It's time for a change of life! Miró resumes his art studies. He is looking for his own style: at first a realist, he then progressively shifts towards a more colourful style influenced by the likes of *Matisse, Monet,* and *Van Gogh**. He fragments reality in the cubist style of Picasso… Do you know these artists?
At 25, Miró shows his work in Barcelona for the first time. He founds La Agrupació Courbet, a group of young artists who are opposed to the *conservatism* in Catalan art.

Conservatism wants to preserve ancient traditions and does not embrace new ideas and progress.

It's your turn! Use the frames to draw the works of your first ever exhibition!

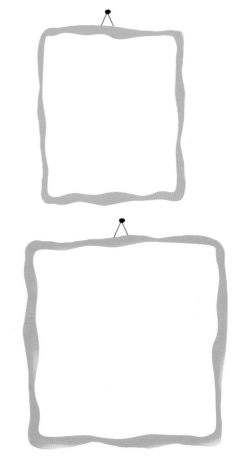

* To learn more about these artists, read *The Little Matisse, The Little Monet* and *The Little Van Gogh* by the same author.

Surrealists!

In 1920, Miró goes to Paris for the first time! He meets painters, writers and poets who, like him, want to "change the world". They are the Surrealists! They want to combine reality and their imaginary world. How do they do this? The hand is allowed to draw or write randomly, freed of rational control. It's called automatic writing and drawing. The young painter is poor: hunger induces hallucinations in him, which he uses as a source of inspiration. Miró finally finds a way of expressing his inner turmoil. He wants to transform the world through poetry.

Be a Surrealist! Take a blank sheet of paper and, without thinking, write down the words that cross your mind and draw imaginary shapes. It produces strange results, doesn't it?

Harlequin

However, Miró does not use this spontaneous approach to paint *Carnaval d'Arlequin*. He draws many preparatory sketches that he annotates. And here's the result!

Can you tell the story of Harlequin?

Look for the details in the painting? The automat playing the guitar, the Harlequin with the big moustache, the insect coming out of the die, two cats playing with a ball of wool, a flying fish, the ladder with an ear, a conical representation of the Eiffel Tower and more...

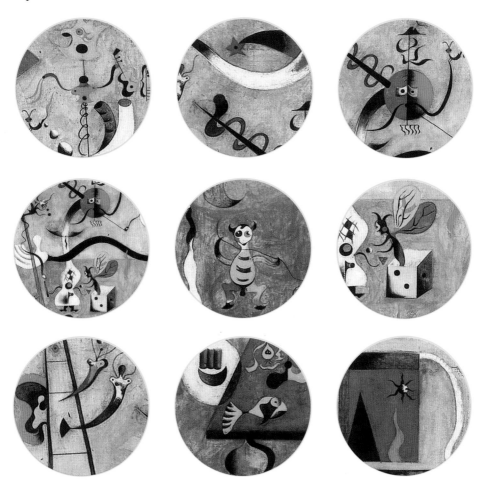

Russian Ballets

Romeo

In 1926, Joan Miró collaborates with the German Surrealist painter and sculptor Max Ernst (1891-1976). They are commissioned to design the sets and costumes for the ballet *Romeo and Juliet* performed by the Ballets Russes, a world renowned ballet company created in 1907 by the Russian Sergei Diaghilev.

In 1932, Miró also designs the sets and costumes for *Jeux d'enfants* ("*Children's Games*"), another ballet produced by the Ballets Russes de Monte Carlo.

In this ballet, toys come to life. Have you heard of similar stories? The artist imagines a backdrop with geometric shapes representing a nursery. The costumes were very modern for the times!

It's your turn! Like Miró, create and draw the nursery of Jeux d'enfants using geometric shapes. The stage is all yours!

Postcard

In 1928 Miró travels to Holland and Belgium. In Amsterdam, he discovers Dutch masters such as Jan Vermeer (1632-1675). He buys postcards of two 17th century Flemish paintings he admires in a museum.

Later that year, he paints his own versions of the paintings, which he calls *Dutch Interior I, II* and *III*. Miró's having fun! He is fascinated by details: he depicts each object in a very precise way. In his paintings he enlarges animals whilst he miniaturises inanimate objects, such as the pitcher. Can you see this?

Compare the painting of Joan Miró (1928) with the original painting by Hendrik Martensz Sorgh (1661). Can you spot the lute player, the dog, the cat, the window with the view of Amsterdam? Which picture do you prefer?

1661

1928

OLÉeee!

The Spanish dancer whirls around and around in her frilly Flamenco dress.
She gracefully raises her arm made of dots!

In this painting can you spot the dancer's comb,
her fan, her dress? Is she playing castanets?

Miró claims "I want to assassinate painting"! He begins a series of collages using simple objects and materials which become poetic compositions. A wooden drafting triangle, sandpaper, bits of rope, hat pins and small bits of paper turn into a dancer!

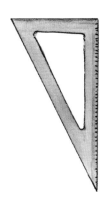 Draw a Spanish dancer using the drafting triangle.

DADA

Congratulations to the newlyweds! In 1929 Miró marries Pilar Juncosa in Palma de Mallorca; the couple moves to Paris. Their only daughter, Dolorès, is born the following year. Joan has his first solo exhibition in New York in 1930. The artist is fascinated by literature and poetry and now seeks to combine several art forms: collage, sculpture, *lithography*, painting, poetry... *Dadaist* poet Tristan Tzara (1896-1963) asks him to illustrate his book *L'Arbre des voyageurs*, for which Joan produces his first lithographs.

Lithography: *method of printing using a stone with a smooth surface.*
A Dadaist *is an artist who challenges the traditions in art. Dadaism is a return to childlike spontaneity.*

Notice the layout of the text and the illustrations.

The Illustrator

In 1932 the family moves back to Barcelona. Joan sets up his studio in the attic of his childhood house. What does he do there? All sorts of collage experiments!

Your turn now! Write a short poem, Dada style, and illustrate it.

- -
- -
- -
- -

Magical shapes

Bright yellow skies. Waves of sand… Evocative shapes in the air and sand…
What do they mean? Miró invents a new vocabulary. Reality disappears.
Circles, cones, lines, dotted lines, letters take over his paintings and appear
like magical symbols.
It is the «mirómonde": an animated world full of signs and *pictograms*. Miró
has developed his own language. And everyone can interpret it as they see fit.

Pictogram: a stylised drawing which acts as a symbol and can replace a word.

Can you spot the geometric shapes, the hunter smoking a pipe, the ladder? What's the ladder used for?

There is a half completed word painted on the picture. Can you complete it? "Sard" as in

....

Miró paints imaginary creatures, «organic» shapes that seem to come to life but aren't real. They are inspired by nature and sometimes take on the appearance of an eye, a huge foot, a bird, insects, stars, distorted planets… A ladder often seems to link the artist's cosmic universe to his native land.

What about you? Can you create your own secret language? Imagine a magical universe. Draw it using pictograms.

The Catalan

Miró is a Catalan at heart and he finds his exile in Paris unbearable. His heart remains in Catalonia, his homeland and his main source of inspiration.
The dry earth, the smell of eucalyptus, the pods hanging from the carob trees, the vast starry skies, but also the faces of the people from the countryside...
He misses all of this!

In this painting, Miró depicts a Catalan peasant. Can you see him? Describe him?

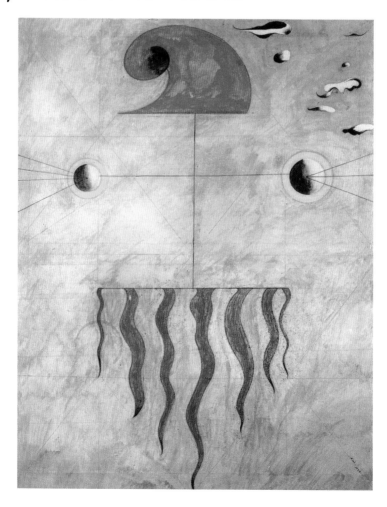

Wild paintings

Miró is a visionary. In 1934, he senses the coming of the war and begins a series of "wild paintings". They are as wild as his torments, with violently contrasting colours, and demons that seem to come straight out of his nightmares, shrieking harrowingly.

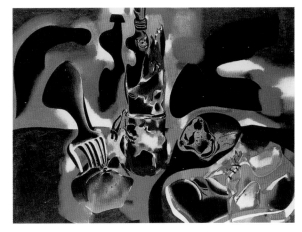

Still life with old shoe

What about you? Would you consider drawing or writing if you were sad? Like Miró, create your "wild paintings" below.

Constellation

In 1940, the war against Germany has just begun. Miró begins his series of
constellation paintings, inspired by the changing skies of Normandy. He needs
to escape into another world. He withdraws into himself and paints a series
of twenty-three gouaches on paper.
What is a constellation? A group of stars forming a shape or pattern in the sky
which has been given a name . Do you know any? The Big Dipper is
one of the famous ones. There are also the twelve signs of the zodiac
(Leo, Taurus, Libra, Scorpio, etc.).

What's your zodiac sign? Draw your
constellation using Miró's style whilst
listening to classical music.

Joan Miró rearranges the cosmos like a music score. He listens to Bach
and Mozart. The earth, planets, suns and stars form a balanced composition
orchestrated by the artist who dives into a new dimension.
Black planets, white moons and blue stars are connected by a fine net.
Can you hear the notes being sung? It is the nightingale's song at midnight.

**Have you ever counted the stars in the sky
at dawn?**

Haiku

In 1966, Miró exhibits in Japan. During his trip there, he discovers the art of *haiku* poetry. Haiku are simple and compact poems that often refer to nature and the seasons. They convey a vivid and evocative message.

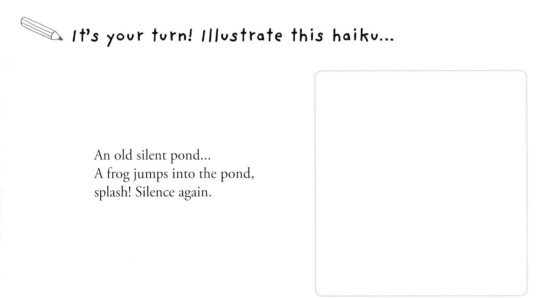

It's your turn! Illustrate this haiku...

An old silent pond...
A frog jumps into the pond,
splash! Silence again.

...And this one in Japanese!

古池や
蛙飛込む
水の音

Miró is introduced to this art by his friend the Japanese poet Takiguchi.
Small details are as important as the main elements. A single stroke on
a monochrome background (that is to say of a single colour), is enough
to convey the emotion. Increasingly, the artist focuses on the essential.
For him, it is more important to paint the forces of nature rather than physical
characteristics (as an example, the flight of the bird or the power of the ox
rather than the animal itself).

What does this painting make you think of?
Make it come to life and tell a story.

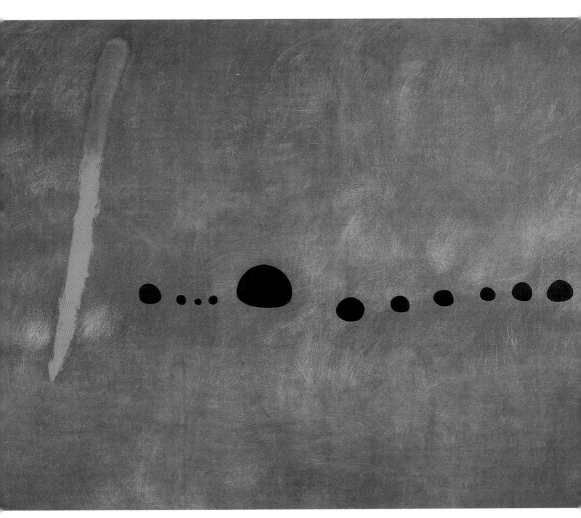

Smile

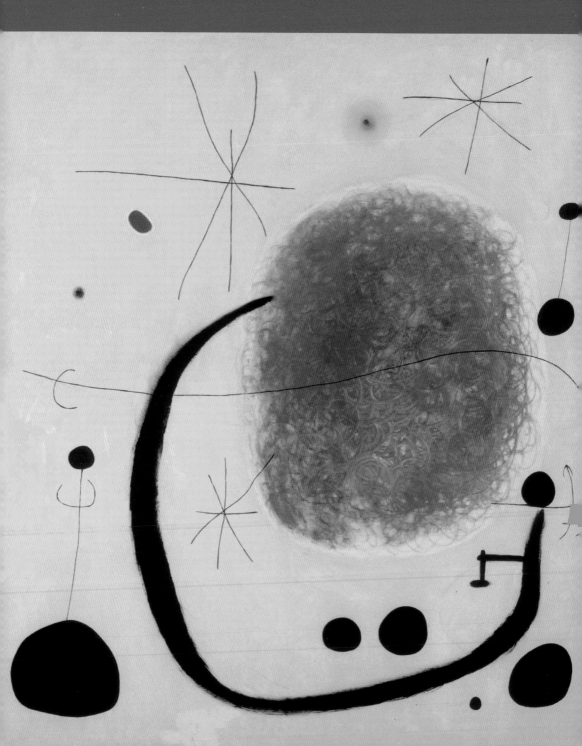

Yellow Red Blue

Miró has gold in his fingers and stars in his mind. In 1967 he completes this dazzling painting, *The Gold of the Azure*. Which planet is this? Have you seen the smile of the crescent moon? What about the myriad stars: is this a new galaxy? Everything seems to be perfectly balanced, just like one of the mobiles by Alexander Calder (1898-1976), the American sculptor and friend of Miró.

The Spanish artist uses several techniques here: a bright yellow background, a big blue oval created by small circular brushstrokes, a large black arc forming a moon, stars made out of thin lines, big black round patches. The white canvas appears here and there.

Miró loves colours. He often uses primary colours, red, yellow or blue. Can you see a touch of green in this painting?

It's your turn! Draw a galaxy on the yellow background.

Woman or bird?

In 1956, Miró moved into a huge empty studio in Palma de Mallorca. He suddenly feels young again. He's 63! The following year, Miró and his friend, the ceramist Artigas, go to Altamira, near Santander to admire the prehistoric cave paintings. The sight of the "first mural painting" of bison inspires them to collaborate on new projects. They work together on many ceramic murals after this landmark visit. Miró likes experimenting with new techniques, constantly renewing himself.

Here is Miró's last work, *Woman and Bird*, a twenty-two metre high sculpture, in mozaic. It stands in a park in Barcelona.

Draw a garden around the monumental Woman and Bird sculpture.

Miró is interested in the representation of women since prehistoric times.
He does some research on the theme of the "bird woman". One of the recurring
themes in his work is women and birds who dance under the moon and the
stars. The woman turns into a mythological bird and links the earth to the sky.
The artist emphasises the importance of a harmonious relationship between
man and nature.

Silence...

"The spectacle of the sky overwhelms me. I'm overwhelmed when I see, in an immense sky, the crescent of the moon, or the sun. There, in my pictures, tiny forms in huge empty spaces. Empty spaces, empty horizons, empty plains - everything which is bare has always greatly impressed me."

Miró aspires to peace and serenity. He is fascinated by meditation and vast expanses. He paints large stretches of colour, like the painter Mark Rothko (1903-1970), reminiscent of inner journeys.

Make up a title for this painting and write it down:

Joan Miró dies at the age of 90 on December 25, 1983 in Palma de Mallorca. He is buried in the Montjuic cemetery in Barcelona. Miró was a prolific artist and leaves a huge legacy: close to 2000 oil paintings, 5000 drawings and collages, 400 sculptures, 400 ceramics and 3500 lithographs, etchings and other works.

Miró.

Text and illustration: Catherine de Duve
Research: Aurore t'Kint
Concept and productions : Kate'Art Editions
Translated by : Antoine de Spoelberch
Proofreading : Kerry-Jane Lowery

With thanks to: Emilio Fernández Miró et Pilar Otego, Succession Miró, Ingrid Fontanet Astudillo, Fundacio Miró, Aurore t'Kint, Carole Daprey, Olivier Olbrechts and everyone who helped to make this book.

Books by Kate'Art Editions are available in various languages:
French, English, Dutch, German, Spanish, Italian, Danish,
Japanese and Russian

Go to www.kateart.com
and its online boutique